AF488393

Night Hunt!
Ryukyu
By
Coco McQ
Illustrated By
Ron Covert

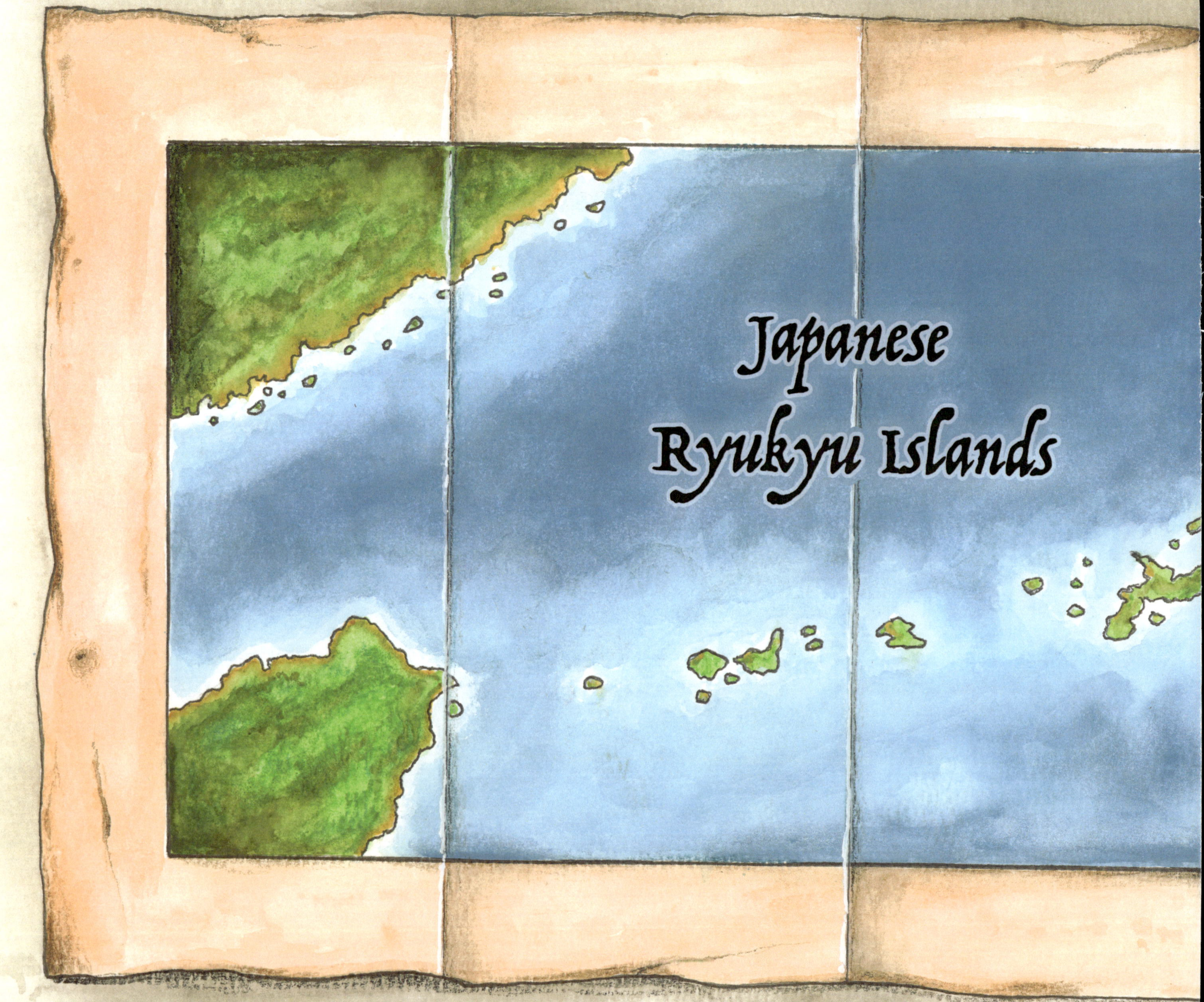

Japanese
Ryukyu Islands

Copyright © 2025 by Coco McQuown
All rights reserved.

No part of this book may be reproduced, stored in a retrieval system, or transmitted in any form or by any means—electronic, mechanical, photocopying, recording, or otherwise—without the prior written permission of the publisher, except in the case of brief quotations embodied in reviews or articles.

Night Hunt! Ryukyu
Written by Coco McQuown
Illustrated by Ron Covert

Published by Sand Dollar Press
Florence, Oregon

First edition, 2025
ISBN: 979-8-9994067-1-2

Printed in the United States of America

Library of Congress Control Number: 2025917331

Cover and interior design by Heather Cash

To learn more visit cocomcq.com

Dedication:

For my amazing and adventurous family,
the inspiration behind it all—this adventure began with you.

Acknowledgements:

Thanks to Melissa Richeson and Rosie Greening for their editorial guidance
and to Curt Peters for his amazing digital skills.

雷中變小 XJ

Ryukyu Islands
Get your flashlight.
Ready? Set!
Let's go hunting
in the dark...
Search out shadows
in the trees...
Find what's clinging
to the bark.

Hot and muggy,
wear long sleeves.
Something buzzes,
tries to bite!
Crawlers, fliers,
stingers... ouch!
Shoo them off—
we'll be alright!

Phew, they're gone—
we made it through!
Let's keep searching,
here we go...
Something rustled...
was it you?
Follow me,
don't walk too slow!

Quick! Beware that shiny web!
Duck down under, scoot away!
Giant hunter swinging low…
Waiting, snagging juicy prey.

Something scaly
slithers by,
Forked tongue flicks.
Oh no! Fangs!
Climbs a rock,
winds up a vine...
Coils that cling,
long tail that hangs.

Hear that chatter
up above?
Something's stirring
from its bed.
Belly full, coat
brushed and cleaned...
Daytime sleeper
once it's fed.

Croakers, chirpers,
evening choir...
Leapers playing
hide and seek!
Padded toes stick
fast to leaves...
Green on green
disguise technique!

Hanging low, eyes
glowing red...
Upside down, waits
for the dawn.
Musky! Scrabble!
Pumping wings!
Flapping through the dark...
it's gone!

Don't get tangled
in the vines!
Point your light!
The path is dark.
Something's out there,
do you hear?
Something's clinging
to the bark.

Splashing, yowling!
Soggy fur...
Small meow-er.
Timid, shy.
Jumper! Scrambling
up the tree...
Master prowler.
Silent spy.

Fading moonlight,
rustling wings...
Screeching, searching
down below.
Gazing backwards,
swooping fast...
Snatching dinner
on the go!

Armor plated,
spiky horns...
Clumsy waddler,
scratching 'round.
Scuffing, scraping,
licking sap
From the roots
along the ground.

Silent glider, jumps, then soars, Parachuting tree to tree... Eyes like marbles scan the dark, Just beneath the canopy.
Let's get back, it's getting late... Find the path to take us home. Keep it lively! Watch your step! Look for critters on the roam.

Sticky jungle.
Twisty vines.
We're done hunting
in the dark.
Moving shadows.
Secret life.
That's what's clinging
to the bark!
小喿中電火丁

Fun Facts

The Ryukyu Islands are a chain of tropical islands in southern Japan, known for their lush jungles, coral reefs, and rare wildlife. When night falls, the jungle comes alive with nocturnal critters on the move.

Here's what we found:

Banana Spider

This spider spins a web that shines like gold in the sunlight! It's called the Golden Silk Orb Weaver, but it's often nicknamed the banana spider for its shape and color.

Mosquito

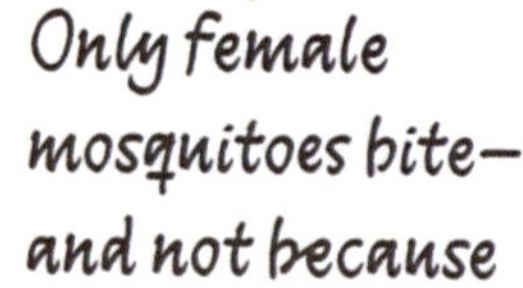
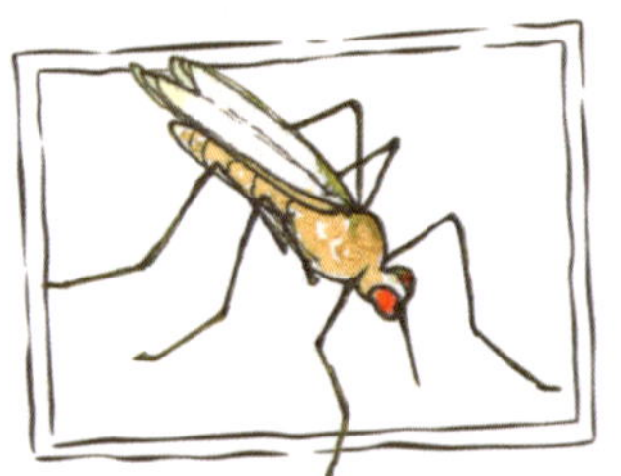

Only female mosquitoes bite—and not because they're mean! They need a little blood to help make their eggs. The rest of the time, they sip nectar like butterflies. They're most active at dawn and dusk, and can smell you from far away!

Ryukyu Giant Rat

This rat climbs trees, sleeps in hollow logs during the day, then wakes at night to search for fruit, seeds, and crunchy bugs. It's one of the largest rats in Japan—with a long tail tipped in white and a nose that's always sniffing for snacks.

Brown Tree Snake

This long, slender snake can climb trees, slip through rafters, and even slither along power lines. It uses its forked tongue to "taste" the air and find its prey.

Green Tree Frog

Tree frogs have sticky toes that help them grip leaves and climb straight up plants.
They're tiny, but they're loud—especially when it rains. At night, they leap from branch to branch, blending in so well you might miss them entirely.

Iriomote Wildcat

This shy wildcat is about the size of a house cat—but much harder to find. It lives deep in the jungle, hunting at night and hiding in rocks or fallen trees by day. It loves to swim, can cross rivers, and eats everything from insects to wild pigs!

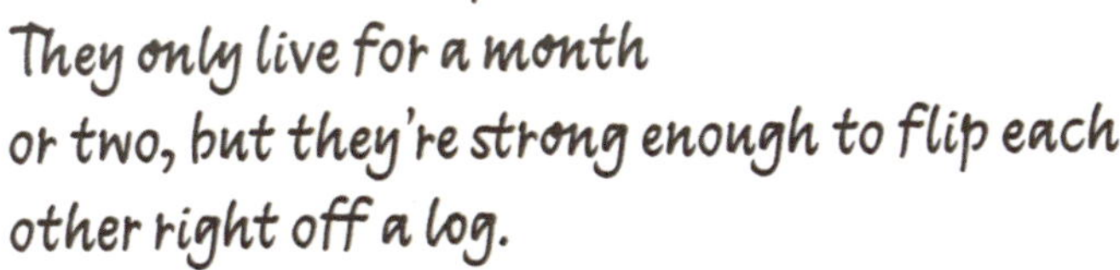

Japanese Rhinoceros Beetle

This beetle has a horn like a tiny triceratops! The males use their horns to wrestle each other for the best tree sap.
They only live for a month or two, but they're strong enough to flip each other right off a log.

Flying Fox

This bat is huge—with wings that stretch longer than your arms! It doesn't use echolocation. Instead, it relies on its eyes and nose to find fruit, flowers, and nectar in the dark. To eat, it crashes into trees, hangs upside down, and snacks using its feet!

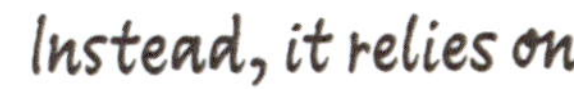

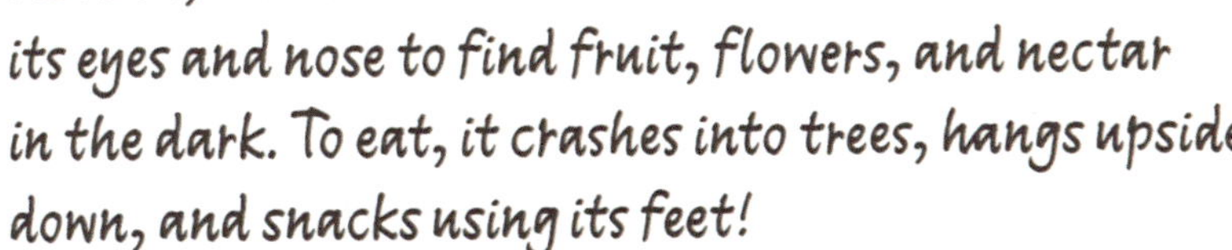

Ryukyu Scops Owl

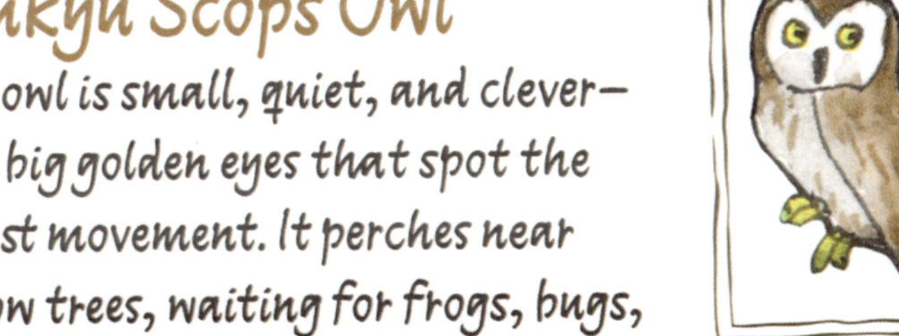

This owl is small, quiet, and clever—with big golden eyes that spot the tiniest movement. It perches near hollow trees, waiting for frogs, bugs, or even other birds to come close.
When it hunts, it doesn't hoot—it whispers on wings through the dark jungle.

Ryukyu Flying Squirrel

This little glider leaps from tree to tree like a parachute with fur! It has big round eyes, a flat tail, and a furry flap between its legs that helps it soar. It sleeps in hollow trees and wakes up when the stars are out, sailing through the branches like a silent shadow.

Adventure begins wherever you are. Go explore!
-Coco McQ

Tales for Curious Minds, Brave Hearts,
and Wild Imaginations

www.cocomcq.com

www.ingramcontent.com/pod-product-compliance
Lightning Source LLC
Chambersburg PA
CBRC101057120726
48010CB00014B/361